The Jaguar Who Went Blind

Elena Marie Santín

Copyright © 2011 Elena Marie Santín

All rights reserved.

ISBN: 061554083X
ISBN-13: 978-0615540832 (COOL-FORCE)

This book is dedicated to my brother Eli.

Thank you Dr. Hipke for your guidance and encouragement.

Once upon a time, there was a jaguar. His name was Tilong. He lived in the rainforest. He was all grown up - 8 years old - so he lived all by himself.

Tilong loved to swim. After he caught his food, he liked to jump into a hot pool in the rainforest. He loved how it felt to use his strong paws to swim through the water.

One day, when he looked into the water, everything was blurry. He felt weird. And when he looked up and around the rainforest, he saw that animals and trees and bushes and vines were also blurry. Now he felt confused.

Every morning everything got darker. And then one morning when he woke up, everything was totally dark all the way. Now he felt scared.

Then Tilong realizes he is blind. Then he smelled something really far away. Then he gets closer to it and finds steak!

Then tiger shows Tilong how to swim. Tiger keeps his front paw on Tilong until they get to the pond. Tilong uses his paws to feel the wetness. Tilong pictures the tiger swimming. And then Tilong gets the hang of it.

Tilong learned he can still use his paws for touch and he can still use his smell. He can smell better when he's blind. Tilong felt VERY happy. He is proud that he can still do stuff even when he is blind.

And now every morning when Tilong wakes up, everything gets lighter and lighter. And then he realizes he can see again. Tilong feels happy.

But Tilong knows that if he is ever blind again he would know he could do things. That makes him feel kind of happy.

THE END

www.ingramcontent.com/pod-product-compliance
Lightning Source LLC
Chambersburg PA
CBHW040032050426
42453CB00002B/97